I0424362

EVERY WOMAN'S JOURNEY

By

Sandra Coldero Gonzalez

Copyright © 1996, 2001 by Sandra Coldero Gonzalez
All rights reserved.
No part of this book may be reproduced, stored in a retrieval system, or
transmitted by any means, electronic, mechanical, photocopying,
recording, or otherwise, without written permission from the author.

ISBN: 0-75963-532-3

This book is printed on acid free paper.

Written & Published by Sandra Coldero Gonzalez

Copyright © 1996 - TXU 786-057 LIBRARY OF CONGRESS AS
EVERY WOMANS' PAIN

1stBooks – rev. 05/02/01

CONTENTS

EVERY WOMAN'S JOURNEY

A woman's journey through life is filled with obstacles,

Obstacles that are continuously placed in her path.

She becomes them, but

has to work twice as hard to achieve her goals.

She is constantly being placed on trial to prove herself,

and the recognition given cannot be compared

to her accomplishments.

In pain, she brings forth man into this world,

Only to be chastised by him.

In love, she marries him,

Only to become a piece of furniture that's rarely used,

with no sense of acknowledgement.

In sickness, she nurses him back to health,

Only to be pushed aside for another.

In sorrow, she pleads with him,

but is shown no mercy.

Women are the driving force that keeps the world turning.

They are the mothers of the world.

Without women the world would be no more,

Yet, they are treated like a useless piece of furniture

that is discarded when they're tired of seeing it.

Every drop of rain that falls is a tear.

Tears that come from every woman's pain.

A pain that is felt in the hearts of every woman.

FOOTPRINTS BY THE SEA

She walks alone on the pale white sand,

leaving only her footprints behind, never looking back,

for fear of what she might see.

Her arms are tightly wrapped around her to keep warm,

but cannot.

She's cold, so cold and cannot be comforted.

She stops for a minute and stares out at the raging sea.

She could see the angry waves crashing into the rocks,

And there, in the midst of it all,

she could see a log being tossed and thrown everywhere

the waves would take it, with never a calm moment.

Then suddenly, without any warning, it stops.

No more tossing and throwing,

but it keeps drifting, slowly drifting alone,

without a destination.

Sandra Coldero Gonzalez

As the log in the middle of the raging sea,

so to was her life, full of excitement, never alone.

But now, she's drifting alone, alone and cold

with no warm memories to reflect upon.

Without a place to call home.

She's searched far and wide seeking a place of serenity

A place to hide from her past, but cannot.

Alas, with nowhere left to turn,

She looks up to the heavens with a silent plea,

A plea to be taken out of her misery.

Without saying a word, Life had ended as she knew it.

CASTLES IN THE SAND

She had spent so many years building and strengthening

the bond that holds her family together.

Doing everything in her power,

To give her family a sound foundation

A foundation so strong, It cushions their fall

on there way up that ladder to success.

There are so many predators today

that prey on breaking the bond that keeps a family together.

It's so unfair, after investing all of your time,

love and life to keeping your family together,

It can be taken away by the blink of an eye.

We cannot control what goes on outside our home.

So we have a sense of fear

when confronted with anything that threatens our family,

or when we feel we are losing control in our home.

It seems as if trying to build a family today

is like building castles in the sand.

It stands straight and tall,

waves crashing to the shore,

never quite reaching it, but gradually

loosening the grains of sand,

weakening the foundation.

Suddenly, without any warning,

an angry wave crashes to the shore,

Destroying that beautiful castle in the sand.

Leaving only a memory of what was.

And no matter how hard you try to rebuild it

It will never be the same.

UNFAIR LOVE

Her love for him can only be,

The eighth wonder of the world.

It is pure and filled with warmth,

like the sun shining upon your face

on a cold winter's morning.

Yet

His love for her is like a rock.

It gives no warmth on cold winter mornings,

or a listening ear, just to show that it cares.

It shows no mercy to anyone.

It only crushes everything in its path.

It is not capable of love, because, it has no heart.

Yet

She gives her love freely to him.

She's always there to lend a listening ear,

or a comforting touch that says:

I love you, and I'll always be here for you.

Yet

His love for her is self-serving.

It's like an aged bottle of wine, it makes you feel good,

but only for a short time. Only, his love dies with age.

Yet

She would give her life to save his,

because a short time of love

can mean a lifetime of happiness to her.

LOVING WITHOUT REASON

She lays next to him every night

Closing her eyes so as not to see his cold eyes.

She loves him more than life itself.

She would do anything for him.

She knows that he's with her only in body.

She could feel it in every touch.

She could see it in his eyes.

But she would rather have him in body,

than not to have him at all.

And hopes one day she will put the sparkle in his eyes,

that's seldom seen.

She understands his feelings,

because she to is loving, without being loved.

The heart is the only part of our body,

we cannot control.

Sandra Coldero Gonzalez

It loves without reason, and gives no warning.

All is never fair in love,

for the one you love,

is rarely, the one that loves you.

LOVE IS

Love is the greatest gift given to man,

It is pure and comes straight from the heart.

Love can be spiritually inspiring,

physically fulfilling and mentally overwhelming, but

How could something so wonderfully inspiring,

cause so much pain and heartache.

How could something so wonderful, be so cruel.

Love is not always fair.

When you love someone and

that love is not returned, or

When the one you love

uses your love for his selfish pleasures and gain.

Love is not always the answer.

Sometimes you have to let go to survive love trials.

Love is sometimes mistaken, and we often suffer needlessly.

11

Love is holding on when you want so desperately to let go.

Love is letting go, when you want so much to hold on.

To live is to love, To love,

even for a short time is worth living.

A MOTHER'S LOVE

In every corner of the world,

Mothers of every creed and race,

have sacrificed their lives

in one way or another to raise their family.

They endeavor to do their best to

provide a sound foundation, so

that their children's lives are well structured.

They are never commended

for this impossible task set before them.

In fact, they are often chastised by the ones they love.

Husbands and children never appreciate a wife or mother

or the things she does, until she's gone.

Rather, they blame her for their shortcomings.

They think that she should submit to their every whim.

Husbands, you should love your wives.

Send her roses just because.

Let her know you love her, and

appreciate the little things she does.

Mothers and wives are the strength of a family.

Without her, the foundation is likely to crumble.

Children, embrace your mothers, and let her know you care.

You may take her for granted,

thinking she will be their forever.

One day you will awake to realize, this is not so.

So give her all the love you can, and

never, never forsake her in her time of need.

A mother's love can never be replaced.

No matter how long you live,

you will never experience a mother's love.

A love that's unconditional, but

know, the wrong you do her, you will live to regret.

MOTHER

Mother, you've given me what no one else can

You're always there to offer a helping hand,

lend a listening ear or give a comforting touch

when no one else cares.

You have showed me an unconditional love.

You have taught me that there are no boundaries in love.

You taught me to respect others and also to respect myself.

When I was a child you nourished my body,

enriched my soul and fed me knowledge.

When I was an infant you stayed up nights,

holding me in your arms,

gently rocking me to sleep,

with no concern or care for yourself.

Sandra Coldero Gonzalez

When I was hurt you took my pain away

with your warm loving touch and words of wisdom,

drying all my tears.

When I was rude and obnoxious

you've always had a firm but gentle way

of making me aware of my shortcomings.

Mother...there is none greater on earth.

You are my hero, I owe all my accomplishments to you

You are the wind beneath my wings.

With all my love

MOTHER

REFLECTION

She lays on the green meadow, staring at the endless skies

Looking at all of nature's natural beauty that surrounds her.

She closes her eyes and could feel the warmth of the sun,

gently shining upon her face, and

the gentle summer breeze that seems to gently caress her body.

With a smile upon her face,

She remembers the warmth of her mother's touch,

and gentle ways of molding her.

She remembers blossoming into a beautiful young lady,

and falling in love with the man of her dreams.

He was everything she had ever wanted,

kind, considerate, understanding and

never afraid to show his love for her.

They were so happy together, it seemed unreal.

He filled every facet in her life.

She was never in want of anything, until

He was taken away by one of life's senseless tragedies.

He loved her so completely when they were together,

that, even now, she feels the warmth of his touch in

everything she does,

the presence of his love that surrounds her

in all of nature's beauty.

A love that will always be with her

to reflect upon in her time of need.

He had filled her life with so much love.

Love that she will hold on to, and stay close to him,

until they are reunited.

REMEMBER WHEN

She sits on the sandy shore of the sea

her arms wrapped around her

staring at the sea in amazement of its still beauty,

intrigued by the way it can change its character

from calm to raged without any warning.

She's reminded of her own life

with the one who holds her heart

His character was that of the seas

She remembers when she was so naive and innocent

and was enchanted by his charm and beauty.

She was not aware of the danger that lurks

beneath the depth of such still beauty

And was stripped of her innocence

and didn't even know it.

She remembers when understanding and honesty

was the key to love and happiness.

She remembers when her life was so simple

Now, like the restless wind that moves the seas

there is an unseen force that pushes her forward

to break the spell cast upon her by this still beauty.

Only then can she live the life that

she can only now remember when...

ILLUSIONS

She walks alone every night, searching,

Searching for something she may never find.

She has searched the hearts of many and

the eyes of others, but,

it seems to no longer exist.

Sometimes she thinks she's found it,

Only to realize that it was just an illusion,

an illusion that soon fades

leaving a feeling of emptiness.

She fears that she too will soon fade,

That her life will not be fulfilling

without experiencing the pleasures

and happiness of true love,

She fears she will be alone and lonely.

Sandra Coldero Gonzalez

Is true love only an illusion

we have created in our minds

to keep us from fading? Or

is it somewhere out there?

We must search diligently to find it.

If we find it, we have to hold on to it

with every breath we take,

Because there is always someone,

Someone who wants to take your happiness away.

TO LOVE COMPLETELY

Through the ages many have tried

to unfold the mysteries of love.

We all have mixed concepts of love

some think love must be shared

with as many partners possible,

Others enjoy sharing their love and life

faithfully, with one partner, but

One's passion can be another's pain.

Love is like drinking your first glass of wine,

It's overwhelming at first, and

some may drink all at once, enjoying that rush,

Others drink slowly, savoring every last drop.

Sandra Coldero Gonzalez

Love affects everyone differently.

It brings out a part of you,

you never knew existed.

It awakens hidden feelings you've never imagined possible.

When you give your love to someone,

You should give all of you,

or none at all.

Men have never been satisfied with one partner.

They think the more partners they have,

The more love they have to give.

Love is sacred, and

should never be used in a sinful manner.

Love must always be given, never taken or demanded.

True love can never be given to two at the same time,

For one will always suffer

To Love Completely

You must devote all of yourself to one partner,

never holding back or sharing with others

Only then, can one truly love completely.

Sandra Coldero Gonzalez

LOVE AND HATE

The world we live in today,

is such a harsh and cruel place.

There's so much hate surrounding us,

They have forgotten how to love.

Their hearts are cold,

therefore can give no warmth.

It makes you wonder,

Will you ever find true love?

If you do, it must be protected,

never taken for granted, and

treasured like a priceless jewel. For

Love can be the greatest healing potion.

Love can also be a disease,

that gradually eats away your will to live,

and love can inflict pain you've never imagined possible.

To hate is so easy, to love is to be forgiving.

There is a fine line between love and hate.

One must be careful never to cross it.

Where there is love, jealousy exists.

When jealousy exists, one is always accused needlessly,

causing pain and heartache.

If you truly love someone,

You must accept them the way they are.

Not try to change them to suit your own needs.

Love is giving freely and

accepting without question, only then

will loving come naturally, and

you will never cross that fine line

between love and hate.

Sandra Coldero Gonzalez

HIDDEN PAIN

She is as graceful as a swan, and

as beautiful as a rose in perfection.

When she walks into a room

her radiance can be felt throughout, and

when she smiles, the world smiles with her.

But, no one knows the agony she feels

deep within the core of her soul.

A pain that eats away at her essence of life.

A pain, she hides so well.

Her touch can be as refreshing as

a gentle summer breeze and

as soft as the kiss of snow.

She is the envy of every woman, and

is desired by every man.

But her heart aches only for the one she loves

A love that can never be returned.

For, it was lost in a battle for life.

CIRCLE OF PAIN

She walks along the pale white sands of the shore

Searching for something she may never find.

She stares out at the sea admiring its still beauty.

She could see a ray of sunlight reflecting on the waters

giving a lustrous shine and a priceless moment of tranquility.

She wonders if she could ever be as calm and content as the seas.

She is so cold and bitter, she's been through so much pain,

and cannot be comforted.

She is searching for a place of serenity.

A place where she can forget all her pain and sorrows.

A place that would renew her strength and faith in love.

A place that seems to only exist in the minds and

hearts of the pure and innocent.

She wants so much to be happy

to not feel the pain that constantly circles her heart.

Pain that has been with her for so long.

She knows now that the only way to find love again

is to leave her pain behind, never looking back

for the mind is a powerful thing and can project illusions,

illusions so real you may want to turn back

only to get caught in the same circle of pain again.

Only then, she will regain here strength and faith in love.

Sandra Coldero Gonzalez

IF ONLY

Everyday she comes home to an empty house.

A house that was once filled with love.

Filled with the happiness and pleasures of everyday family life.

Happiness that cannot be measured.

If only she could turn back the hands of time.

If only she could change her past.

She would not have taken everyday for granted,

but accepted it as a gift.

A gift given to her out of love from her creator, and

live it to the fullest, that life had to offer.

She was once hurt by one she had let into her heart.

Since then, she's built a wall around her,

never letting anyone in.

She has lived her life alone for

fear of reliving that pain.

Now in her golden years

She wonders, was it all worth it,

Giving up her whole life for a man who

used her for his own pleasures, then

left her alone and unprotected in a lions' den.

She had held on to that pain all her life,

A pain that ruined her chances

of ever finding happiness again,

If only...

Sandra Coldero Gonzalez

REACHING OUT

All her life she's had to settle for less.

She was never given anything.

Rather, what little she had was taken away.

Still, she will help anyone just for the asking.

She would never intentionally hurt anyone.

So why does she suffer needlessly.

I know it's wrong to question one's destiny,

But, Lord, you know her heart's desire.

You know that she is every thing that is pure and true.

Why not raise your hands against the ones that persecute her.

I don't mean to question your will.

It's just so hard watching the

people you love suffer, day after day.

It seems like the closer one gets to the Lord

the more they are persecuted on earth.

Our faith is constantly being put to the test

If you have as little faith as a grain of sand

You can accomplish anything.

Without faith in our creator,

we are like lost sheep without a shepherd.

She has always had faith

and believes that God is with her,

and has been with her all her life,

walking with her, talking with her, even carrying her

when her burden was too much to bear.

Sometimes we lose faith, and

begin to be consumed by the vanities of life.

It seems so natural that,

We don't realize that we are drowning

Sandra Coldero Gonzalez

> *And grasping at straws.*
>
> *We don't see that rope in front of us,*
>
> *All we have to do is reach out*
>
> *and we will be saved.*

UNSPOKEN

Everyday she goes to a little cafe over-looking the lake.

She would spend hours just looking at it.

Trying to forget the pain that surrounds her.

Trying to find something of beauty

and tranquility to hold on to,

To forget, even for a moment.

She felt someone gently caressing her back

She turned to find an old friend.

She looked at him with teary eyes that seem to say

Please take me in your arms.

He held her gently in his arms,

There were no words spoken,

Yet, it's as if he felt her deepest pain,

and knew her every thought.

It's as if he'd never left her

Sandra Coldero Gonzalez

She held on to him as if she was

holding on for life.

It's been so long since she had been held like this,

and felt a moment of calm, after so many storms.

A moment of content she did not want to end.

He would take her away in a second.

But she knows that she has to let go.

Let go of the pain that preys on her life.

A pain that had scarred her heart so deeply.

She will treasure this moment,

and hold it close to her heart.

A moment she will never forget or may never feel again.

She will hold on to it,

to keep her hopes and dreams alive.

DINNER FOR TWO

She sits at the dinner table set for two,

dressed in beautiful black eveningwear, and waits.

Waiting patiently for the one she loves.

Waiting and hoping that maybe, just maybe, this time

he will live up to his word.

He promised that tonight would be different.

That tonight he will be here.

She glances at the clock on the wall.

It is now 7:00 o'clock, and she's still waiting,

waiting and hoping.

She stares at the burning flames on the candlesticks.

She could see the passion he once felt for her in his eyes.

A passion that could keep these candles burning all night.

A passion, that died so long ago.

She glances at the clock on the wall again, and

felt a sharp pain circling her heart.

A pain that bring tears to her eyes.

Tears that she can no longer control.

She got up from her chair at the dinner table,

blew out the candles, her teary eyes glanced at the clock

It was now 10:30.

She can no longer live with this pain

A pain, that shows no mercy.

A pain that crushes her heart

Every time she tries to go an extra mile.

A pain she must leave behind

so she may have a happy tomorrow.

UNQUENCHABLE THIRST FOR LOVE

Life has been very unkind to her.

She's had an uphill battle,

ever since she could remember.

As a child she had to settle for

the bear necessities in life.

Not that she wanted material things, but

There was just a sense of emptiness surrounding her.

Maybe its because she had suffered the loss of her father

at a very tender age. Since then

She had spent her life trying to satisfy

her unquenchable thirst for love.

A thirst that is so great, that

the more is given, the greater her desires become

Each time being compared with that of her father's.

Always know whenever one compares, one is always condemned.

She has searched far and wide, but

her hunger is greater than she can consume.

After relentless efforts to replace her father's love.

She has now discovered the one place

that was untouched in her quest.

The one place, that is so close,

yet so far, her heart.

She had held so much pain in her heart,

that she could never let anyone in.

She has learned that in order to love,

you must first find peace within yourself,

and let go of all the pain you hold inside

Then, and only then can you truly love, and

have a fulfilling life,

For the heart that cannot love,

is a heart that has never lived.

INNOCENCE AND DECEPTION

She is as gentle as a lamb

and as beautiful as a rose in bloom.

She is so young and naive

and does not realize that

she is in the midst of so many thorns.

Thorns can be well hidden.

The eyes can rarely see past

the beauty of a rose in perfection.

He was as handsome and cunning as

a wolf in sheep's clothing.

He walked with her and talked with her.

Deceiving her,

winning her heart with his sophisticated charm.

He thrived on her youth and innocence.

Sandra Coldero Gonzalez

He waited until she was completely absorbed in him

and at the mercy of his deceptive love.

Then, without any warning,

led her away from the flock

devouring her virtue and innocence without mercy.

Without any remorse,

returns to the flock in disguise

and deceives yet another innocent rose.

THE SOUNDS OF SILENCE

She drove past the moonlit lake

admiring its pure, natural and untouched beauty

and long for its peace and tranquility.

Her life had been filled with excitement,

never a dull moment.

She had traveled the world and back again,

she had dinned with queens, slept with kings

and drank with sailors.

She had been given diamonds and rubies.

She's never wanted for anything — until now.

Now, that her nights are empty, cold and long.

She longs to be held — to wake up in someone's arms.

She longs to feel the movement of her unborn child in her womb.

Something she has given up time and time again.

Sandra Coldero Gonzalez

Now, she would give up all the diamonds and rubies

just to hold her unborn child in her arms,

or to feel its warmth against her breast.

She yearns to hear the sound of its little feet

or the touch of its tiny hands gently touching her face.

If only, if only she could turn back the hands of time.

Now, she lies on her bed alone and cold

with not even the comfort of warm memories.

All she can do, is listen,

listen to the sounds of silence

and in the midst she could hear

a baby's cry and the sound of tiny feet around her.

VOICES IN THE WIND

She walks along the green meadow

and could feel the wind gently caressing her body.

She could feel the warmth of the sun gently shining upon her face.

Now and then, she could hear the wind whistling,

as if gently whispering words of love in her ears.

She could see a breath-taking garden of wild flowers

swaying too and fro, as they fragrance the air by

performing an exotic dance of some sort and are driven by

the innocence of one of nature's gift to all — the wind.

If you listen carefully,

you can hear so many voices in the wind.

you can hear laughter, you can feel love.

You can see a flower in bloom and feel its joy,

or you can see a flower wilting and feel its pain.

You can hear a bird singing a love song

and feel its joy or sadness.

47

She comes to this meadow to remind herself that there is still

love and beauty in this wretched world.

As long as we have life, we should have hope,

because there are so many wondrous sounds around us,

all you have to do is listen,

listen to the voices in the wind

Just listen...

WHAT ABOUT HER

Everyday she wakes up at the break of dawn.

Ensuring her family's safety and well being.

She makes sure everyone is cared for.

Then she's on her way to work.

While he sleeps.

She comes home after a stressed day,

prepares and serves dinner.

While he is out having fun and

does not return 'til the break of dawn,

She's left alone, alone again,

With no one to comfort her or

just to hold her in his arms.

She has willingly given up a life of freedom,

for a life raising a family.

She never dreamed she would have to do it alone.

49

She's always there when needed.

Always giving, never asking anything in return.

But what about her?

Who takes care of her?

Who makes sure she's being cared for?

Why is she the one always giving, never receiving?

Was it her destiny to live this way?

Is there some unseen force that chose her fate,

or was there a twist of fate sometime in her life.

She will never know, but

She lives not for pleasures of the earth, but

for eternal happiness that one can never take,

It must be given onto them.

LONGING

She lays on her bed every night

with a gleam of hope in her eyes.

Hoping that tonight would be the night.

The night he would lay beside her,

just holding her in his arms, and

whisper sweet nothings in her ear.

But it is as always.

All she could hear is the opening and shutting of the door,

that seems to drive a knife into her heart,

that creates pain so deep, one can never prepare.

She longs to feel the strength of his arms around her,

the length of his body along side hers,

the tenderness of his touch she once knew, or

the warmth of his lips gently pressing against hers.

Sandra Coldero Gonzalez

She remembers a time when all of this was.

When they were truly happy and inseparable.

That was so long ago, but

she remembers as if it were yesterday.

She remembers their long evening walks on the beach,

hand in hand.

She remembers when they could speak for hours

about anything or nothing at all,

or, just enjoy the other's silent presence.

She holds these memories close to her heart,

for fear of losing

the only true happiness she has ever known.

She has learned that if you want something bad enough

You have to let it go, and

If it comes back to you

It will be yours for all time.

VALLEY OF THORNS

She sits against the wall with her knees under her chin,

Rocking back and forth.

Feeling like the walls are closing in on her, and

There's no where to run or hide.

She wonders why her life has been filled with so much pain,

and when will it end, if ever.

Whenever she feels like she's being released from one,

another is placed upon her shoulders to carry.

If she could cut the pain out from her heart, she would.

Sometimes it's just too much to bear.

She asks: Why have thou forsaken me Lord?

Why me Lord?

What have I done to deserve this unbearable pain?

All my life I've always tried to be the best that I can.

Why am I placed in this valley of thorns to tread upon?

53

Always know that the Shepherd never abandon's his sheep.

His work is slow, but sure.

Your pain and suffering comes from an evil force,

trying to persuade you to forget your values and turn to him.

Keep love in your heart for your creator and

reach out and somewhere, somehow,

the Lord will send you a lifeline.

SILENT PAIN

She sits alone every day

and looks out her bedroom window.

She looks at the flowers in bloom, but sees nothing.

All she could see is an image,

an image of the man she loves,

walking out her door every night.

Her heart will be broken 100 times

before the break of dawn.

She could hear the birds singing, and

the rain drops tapping against her windowpane,

But does not listen.

All she could hear, over and over in her mind

are words so painful, it cuts like a knife,

and the slamming of the door in her face.

She could feel the sunshine gently shining upon her face,

but does not recognize its warmth.

She cannot even feel the warmth of her baby's hand

gently caressing her cheeks.

All she could feel is the pain that circles her heart,

a pain so deep, that she can no longer control

the tears gently running down her cheeks.

Why? Why does she have to suffer such needless pain?

Is it because she has accepted this way of life, or

Is it because the love she feels is so great

that she would choose to endure a life full of pain,

rather than to live a life without him, or

Is it that she feels that one day her pain

will be over, or

Has she chosen to place her life

in the hands of her creator.

The only giver of true love and happiness.

ABUSIVE HANDS

She hurries home,

heart pounding, hands trembling,

glancing at the time.

She's a few minutes late.

She fearfully opens the door

and sees him standing before her,

waiting, with blood-shot eyes.

Before she can begin to explain

his hand comes down on her

like the strike of lightening,

With no mercy for her, or

concern for the teary innocent eyes upon them, and

keeps on striking, until he is satisfied.

Now, she lays helplessly on the floor, sobbing,

with tiny innocent hands gently stroking her hair.

Sandra Coldero Gonzalez

She painfully and slowly sits up to comfort her children.

Holding them tightly in her arms,

She looks at their innocent little bodies.

Realizing that she must get away from

those abusive hands.

If not for herself, but for her children.

For fear that one day

he will raise his hands against them.

While he's sleeping off his anger and liquor.

She crawls to the telephone,

finger reaching out.

It was time to put an end to those abusive hands.

DEEP WITHIN

She has been with him for so long,

So long so, that she cannot remember life without him.

He has put her through so much pain,

So much so, that her pain seems to be a way of life

she has accepted,

He has emotionally raped her,

and stripped her of her dignity,

He has abused her mentally and verbally.

He has taken advantage of her genuinely pure and true nature.

She has tried so many times to put an end

to this selfish relationship, but without success.

Her fondest memories are those of her children.

They are the only true joy and happiness in her life.

They are her reason to get up every morning,

They are, her will to live.

She would no longer exist without the love of her children.

Her life has been filled with pain and unhappiness.

But through it all, she has always kept her head high,

and never gave up hope of being blessed with true happiness,

Something most people take for granted.

She tries her best to accomplish her goals.

Her greatest accomplishments

have been driven by her deepest pain.

She has accomplished so much in life, and yet so little.

For she has yet to accomplish and experience

true love from the man she loves.

She feels deep within her heart that,

Someday she will be loved the way she should be.

She knows now that for someone to be truly happy,

They have to let go of all the pain

and anger they hold inside.

For if true happiness comes from deep within the soul.

Your happiness can only be disrupted,

but never, never taken away.

THORNS AND ROSES

He stood out from all the rest.

He was like a bright shining star

that caught her eyes, the moment she saw him.

He promised her the moon and the sun.

He promised her the world on a golden platter.

He was the cream of the crop,

He was the love of her life.

But no one told her that,

a beautiful rose such as this

is filled with thorns.

No one told her that when in love,

Pain is almost sure to follow.

No one told her that,

a diamond can have many flaws.

She was abused because of her innocence.

She placed her heart in his hands,

he cut it into tiny pieces,

then threw it back to her.

Leaving her to put the pieces together again.

She was blinded by love.

She could not see past the sparkle,

until it lost its shine.

He no longer stands out in a crowd.

She could feel the prick of each thorn.

She's learned that,

everything that sparkles is not a diamond,

and never be fooled by fool's gold.

Sandra Coldero Gonzalez

TEMPTATION

She sits on the bed waiting,

Waiting for him to walk in.

She's sacred, so scared she's trembling.

—She wishes she had never shown—

He walked into the bedroom and

sees her sitting on the bed,

with a look of fright on her face.

But shows no mercy.

She had forgotten all of her values

Her body was telling her to give in

Her heart was pounding and confused

Her head was telling her to escape

He was now standing before her.

He pulled her to her feet, then to him.

She could see the fire burning in his eyes,

that would not be extinguished.

She tries to break free, but cannot.

He seemed to have cast a spell on her.

She's frozen.

She feels his eyes piercing deep into her soul.

She silently pleads, but he does not submit.

With tears gently running down her cheeks.

She looks at him with a silent plea to be set free.

but does not acknowledge.

She violently breaks free from his strong, masculine arms,

and escaped the claws of temptation.

Sandra Coldero Gonzalez

EVERY MAN'S GAIN — EVERY WOMAN'S PAIN

At some point in every mans' life,

if not all his life, he uses women.

He uses women to boost his own ego

and has no regard or respect for the pain a woman feels.

Each time they hurt a woman

They gain respect from their piers.

Each time they hurt a woman

they gain notches on their belt, or

think it grows another hair on their chest,

Every time they break a woman's heart,

they shatter part of her dreams without a care.

The woman is left alone to pick up the pieces,

and deal with her loss and sense of rejection.

A loss that can never be replaced.

There is a part of her that will always feel empty.

A part that will be lost forever.

Women place their heart and trust in man,

only, to see it destroyed for the

sheer pleasures and pride of male ego.

Women lose their dignity,

their willingness to trust another,

sometimes even their virginity,

for a senseless act

committed in male bonding due to selfish pride,

and is scared for life.

Men just move on, and prey on another victim,

feeling like they have just won a lottery,

with no remorse for the woman they left behind,

or the pain they have inflicted on her

For every man's gain evolves around every woman's pain.

Sandra Coldero Gonzalez

BODY & SOUL

They walk along the sandy shore

of the seas, hand in hand.

Her eyes are only for him.

Her heart beats only with his.

His eyes meet with every other eyes he could see.

His heart beats to the sways and curves

of their bodies.

Her thoughts are only of him,

holding him, loving him and

being with him only.

She is with him in mind, body and soul.

He is with her only in body.

His mind, heart and soul belongs

to every wondering soul that is willing.

Willing to give a moment of pleasure.

True love is very sacred.

It should never be used for one's gain.

In turn, causing the other so much pain.

True love is the greatest gift given to man.

When a woman gives her heart to you,

She is giving you everything she holds sacred,

She is giving you her life.

It should not be used as a doormat,

It should be returned with the honesty and purity

with which it was given.

Sandra Coldero Gonzalez

THE OTHER WOMAN

They met and fell in love at a very tender age

She was so much in love

that nothing else mattered.

She built her world around him.

She would do anything for him and his love

For a while, she was the only thing that mattered in his world.

He could not bear the thought of living without her.

His desires were to be with her and her alone; UNTIL,

The other woman came into his life.

She came into his life like a thief in the night,

and stole his heart, not because she wanted it, but

because it belonged to someone else.

She was cold, ruthless and uncaring.

She turned his life upside-down and shattered his family's dream

to satisfy her own thirst and hunger for passion,

that lasts as long as a vapor rising into the air.

His true love was in so much pain,

trying to pick up the pieces of her life,

that was once full of love and happiness.

A life she thought would never end.

After his infatuation with the dark side of love

He returns, seeing her was like a breath of fresh air, or

seeing a flower bloom right before his eyes.

Her love for him was so strong that she just stood there,

with her arms open wide, waiting to embrace him,

even though he made a mockery of their love and commitment.

He knows their lives will never be the same again, and

it is up to him to gain her trust and to

prove to her that he is worthy of having her love.

Sandra Coldero Gonzalez

WHEN A MAN HURTS A WOMAN

What happens to a woman,

When her husband finds love and

comfort in the arms of another?

What happens to a woman,

When she's pushed aside

for someone younger?

What happens to a woman

when she's no longer desired

by the man she married?

The man she made a commitment,

To love and to hold,

in sickness and health, for better or for worse.

What happens when she decides to

stay for better or for worse.

He cannot comprehend, what he did to her

has affected every facet of her life.

He cannot understand that

a woman cannot forget infidelity easily, if ever.

He cannot understand that

he has left a permanent scar on her heart.

He regrets what he has done,

but it doesn't make her recovery any easier.

Some never do, causing both to go their separate ways.

Whenever he touches her,

She can no longer feel his warmth.

His touch is cold and uncaring.

All she could feel is pain.

Pain that seems to constantly pierce her heart.

Every time she looks at him,

and sees him in the arms of a faceless woman.

Still, he wonders why.

Why she no longer reacts the way she used to

with his touch.

Now, he has to prove to her,

That his love is true, and

that he's truly faithful to her,

and that he truly regrets his infidelity and

deserves the right to regain her love and trust.

WOMEN — BUILDERS OR DESTROYERS

Why do we hurt each other?

Why can't we live in harmony?

When will we learn to respect each other as women.

When respect is given it is also obtained.

Women are supposed to be the builders of the world

Not the destroyers.

A woman should never destroy another.

Why would any woman knowingly sleep with another's husband.

Is it for money, is it for power

— true power comes from within,

and cannot be gained by sexual pleasures.

Is it for a mere 30 minutes of pleasure.

You can take away a lifetime of happiness in that 30 minutes of pleasure

or lust.

Sandra Coldero Gonzalez

Is that what you want? Is it really?

I hope not — because one day

you will also feel that sword piercing your heart.

For everyone who lives by the sword,

shall die by the sword.

We are all women and we have all experienced pain

in one form or another.

If we stand together we shall achieve our goals.

We have a responsibility to ourselves

to save our family — not destroy them.

Alone you are just one voice, but

together there is nothing we cannot conquer.

Our voices will be heard and we shall prevail.

We have come a long way to still be dictated to by man.

All you have to do is say no.

Yes it's true, we are living in a mans' world.

We have to speak twice as loud

and work twice as hard for us to obtain recognition.

But that does not mean we should demean ourselves or

lose our self-respect to gain power.

We are worth so much more.

All we have to do is believe in ourselves.

There will be nothing left for our children.

Our children's lives will be one filled with pain and

they will not know the value in showing respect for others.

We live for our family.

Our whole life is based on raising and nurturing a family.

No mother wants to see her children suffer.

We have to learn to say NO! to man.

Then the other woman would become obsolete.

Men, if you dare to look at another woman with lust,

Remember how you felt when you first saw your wife,

Remember the passion that ran through your veins.

Sandra Coldero Gonzalez

Remember how beautiful she looked in that red dress.

Buy her a dozen roses and

take her in your arms and tell her how much you love her,

and that you will do it all over again just for the asking.

If you want out — tell her so — don't be less of a man

and take the easy way out.

You made a vow to love and to hold — to forsake all others

'til death do you part.

You owe it to her,

you owe it to yourself to be honest at the least;

We have to keep our values, We must respect ourselves,

and never settle for less.

We all deserve to be loved completely for what we are

not who we are, or what someone thinks we should be,

and that love should be given to one only

and not shared with any.

A WOMAN'S HEART

A woman's heart is the most delicate part of her body.

It should always be handled gently, and with the utmost of care.

One should never intentionally hurt it.

Yet, so much pain is constantly being inflicted on it.

Every woman's pain stems straight from her heart.

Such pain should never be taken for granted.

A woman's heart can be so easily broken,

and so hard to mend, if ever.

Every woman's pain is inflicted by one she loves,

Sometimes the one she loves has no regard for her pain.

They have no respect for a woman's heart,

A heart that can only give warmth and love to the one it loves.

A woman's heart can be touched so easily,

yet you cannot feel it.

It can feel, but it cannot be felt.

It can be heard in the quiet of the night,

but cannot be seen, but you know it's there.

Maybe that's why the ones we love have

no respect or regard for the pain inflicted on it.

They do not believe in what they cannot see.

Because it seems like there is no end to the pain inflicted upon;

A Woman's Heart.

FORBIDDEN

She has been married for so long,

And has always been faithful, without any effort.

They have managed to raise a family together

Now, they're on their own again.

Something she had been looking forward to,

but he is always so busy and

seems to be caught up in his own world.

They never spend any time together anymore.

She's been alone and so lonely, Until

She met a stranger.

A stranger who brought her back to life.

Someone who's reminded her how it feels to be alive

and always there to lend a listening ear.

Sandra Coldero Gonzalez

She finds herself being drawn to him,

like there is an unseen magnet that keeps

pulling her closer and closer to him.

And there is nothing she can do to stop it.

He makes her feel loved and needed,

Something she needs desperately.

She loves her husband very much

and does not wish to hurt him.

but he has deserted her in her time of need

and left a gaping void that must be filled.

But she can't go on like this

For it is forbidden to love carelessly,

Or can she?

Men have been doing it for centuries.

Forbidden love can be the sweetest

But can also be as bitter as wormwood.

UNFORGETTABLE

She sits and waits in anticipation,

Hoping this will be the end of her journey.

A journey that was filled with pain and heartache.

She waits, and remembers one special night.

A night filled with warmth and magic.

The night she was swept of her feet,

by her knight in shining armor.

A night that she had held on to all her life,

in her quest for happiness.

She remembers spending the evening together,

looking at the setting sun.

They laid innocently on the green meadow,

looking at the starlit sky and its still beauty.

They danced the night away,

under the stars and the moon without a care.

That was the happiest night of her life.

She felt like she had found her soul mate,

This was the missing link in her life.

That was the only time in her life.

she was completely happy and content.

Now, they are meeting again after such a long time.

She feels as if it's the beginning,

or the end of her hopes for happiness.

Their eyes meet, he reached out, held her hands.

It's as if they were touching hearts

It's as if they were never apart.

Now her relentless quest for happiness has ended.

Due to that one unforgettable night, she held on to

and followed her heart.

SPARKLES IN HER EYES

She sits on her porch

looking at the children playing

and remembers her own childhood

Her childhood was built around her mother

Her goal was making her mother happy

She would save every last penny

To buy her mother gifts

Just to see that sparkle in her eyes

Sparkles that had the power to bring you to tears

Now she's grown and has children of her own

there is so much distance between them

that it's so hard to show her mother

the love she deserves

Sandra Coldero Gonzalez

Sometimes we get caught in our own world and

very often we tend to forget kindness

or take it for granted

especially from our love ones

I want to do so much, but

There isn't anything that I can do or give

that can compare with what she has given me.

All I can do is try to make her as happy as she can be

for when she's happy it's so easy to see

that sparkle in her eyes.

MY MOTHER MY FRIEND

Mother, throughout my life you have always been there for me.

You have always led me through the straight and narrow road,

even when I was headed for the wide way of destruction.

I know I may not have always appreciated it,

but now, being a mother myself, has shown me a new light and

I am glad you stood your grounds and didn't spare the rod

when I was being a selfish brat.

I understand now, that you have always been my

only true friend.

A friend who would do anything for me,

even lay her life down for my own.

I know you wanted to make available to me

all the opportunities that was not made available to you,

so that I can be the best that I can be.

I know now how hard it must have been for you,

raising your family on your own

with the added stress and pressures of society.

I have the deepest respect for you mother,

and for all that you have done for me.

Mother - if I could give you the moon and the stars,

I would, just for the asking

I know you deserve the finest of things,

nothing less will do.

You have accomplished raising your children on your own.

You should be commended for this impossible task,

you are my hero.

I am what I am today because of you, Mother.

Your selfless acts and unconditional love still guide me

and gives me the strength and courage I need to be a wife

and mother in today's harsh and cruel world.

I could always count on you being there for me.

Mother, you are the wind beneath my wings

that will take me as high as I could fly.

Mother - there is none greater on earth,

and today, I want to give you a little of what you gave me.

I want to give you the greatest honor

a daughter can give to her mother

and that is the love and respect for others you have instilled in me,

I give it to you wholeheartedly and unconditionally.

Mother, you are one in a million - THANK YOU,

MY MOTHER MY FRIEND

Sandra Coldero Gonzalez

RENEWED TRUST

She was a devoted wife and mother

Who had been continually hurt

by the man she loved and trusted.

A man who betrayed every commitment he made,

Over and over again.

her pain was so intense that

it controlled all of her emotions.

She felt cold and uncaring.

Until her passion was unexpectedly awaken by a stranger,

Everyday she would see him passing by, and

everyday her heart beat quickens.

Each time she sees him,

she feels a fire burning deep within her soul.

And only the warmth and tenderness of his touch

can put out her fire.

She longs to be tenderly kissed by him,

To be gently held in his arms,

to feel his body wrapped around hers

feeling his heart beat with hers,

igniting the flow of passion through her veins

and renewing her trust in love.

Something she thought she would never feel again.

Sandra Coldero Gonzalez

HOLD ON TO YOUR DREAMS

Her life had been filled with trials and tribulations.

As an infant she was placed in the cold hands of a stranger.

She had no place to call her home.

She would be taken from hand to hand,

each being unkind.

She had never experienced the magic of true love.

As an adult she took chances on love and lost.

All she had was the warmth and love of her children.

By the grace of God's love

they have grown and are now on their own.

Why has life been so unkind to her?

She has always tried to be the best that she can be,

Always giving, never asking anything in return.

Sometimes it seems like the things we want most in life,

are the things that are never in our reach.

All she wanted was a happy family life.

We cannot always understand why things happen the way they do.

I do know that we have to believe and place

our undoubted trust in our creator and when a window closes,

always know that a door is being opened somewhere.

We may not always be able to see it,

but know, that it is there,

and will be shown to us

when we are ready to face what's behind.

You must believe, never give up hope and always,

Always, hold on to your dreams.

Sandra Coldero Gonzalez

SECRET DESIRES

She bumped into a gentleman.

He held her by the waist, to protect her fall

Their eyes met briefly, but

it felt like they were touching hearts.

She felt as if he saw her secret desires

and her hidden pain.

She felt like an open book before him.

He was tall, slender, with dark hair and nicely dressed.

He tipped his hat still looking deep into her eyes

and in a deep rouged voice

that seemed to penetrate her soul, said: "Pardon me."

He kept on his way, leaving a hint of cologne around her,

And a memory of his eyes piercing through her soul.

Her heart was pounding just looking at him.

He seemed to have cast a spell on her

She kept on looking

as the sunlight silhouetted his white suit,

Until, they became one.

Strangely enough she feels a sense of loss and

suddenly feels melancholy.

She finds herself wondering

Will she ever see him again.

She feared that this stranger had stolen her heart.

Is this possible, to see someone for the first time

and know at that instance that you have fallen in love?

She's returned to that location numerous times

hoping to see him again

But without success.

Finally, she said she had to put an end to this love affair

with her hopes and dreams of a brief encounter.

She visited the location once more

still he's no where in sight, but

there's always a hint of his cologne around her.

In despair, she turns to return home and

finds herself standing before him,

looking into his piercing eyes that sees her soul

and in that penetrating voice he said.

"I've loved no one else but you"

Held her in his arms and gently pressed his lips against hers

igniting a flame and the flow of passion running through

her veins like a restless sea on a stormy night.

ABOUT THE AUTHOR

Sandra Gonzalez was born and grew up in the Island of Trinidad in the West Indies where she also received her education. She migrated to the United States to join her husband. Since then Philadelphia, Pennsylvania has been her home. She has two daughters and maintains a household for her family and is employed as a Legal Secretary for a major law firm in Center City, Philadelphia. Writing poems for her is therapeutic.

www.ingramcontent.com/pod-product-compliance
Lightning Source LLC
Chambersburg PA
CBHW030347290526
45785CB00004B/1628